Uncharted, Unexplored, and Unexplained

Scientific Advancements of the 19th Century

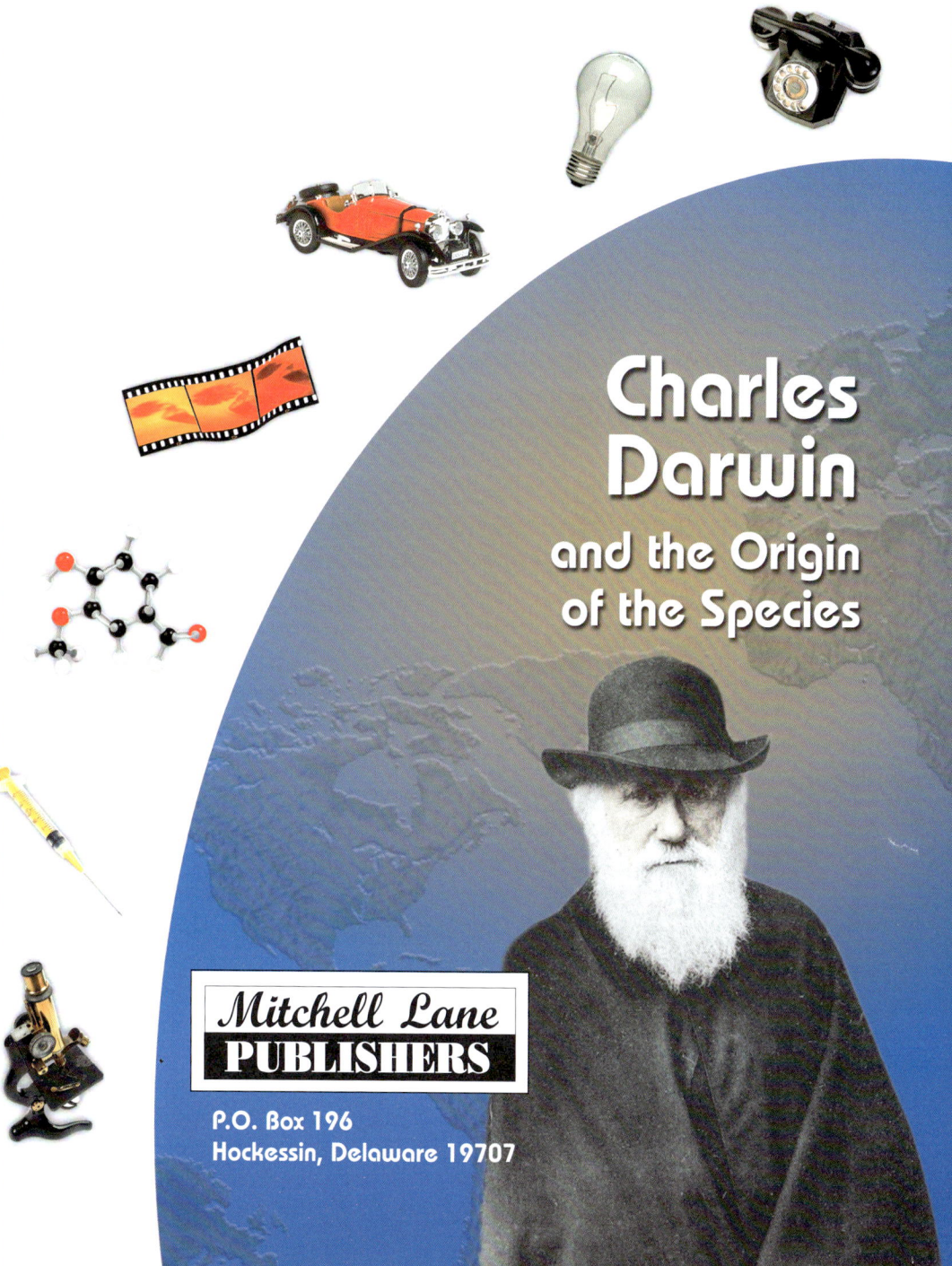

Charles Darwin
and the Origin of the Species

Mitchell Lane PUBLISHERS

P.O. Box 196
Hockessin, Delaware 19707

Uncharted, Unexplored, and Unexplained
Scientific Advancements of the 19th Century

Titles in the Series

Alexander Graham Bell and the Story of the Telephone
Antoine Lavoisier: Father of Modern Chemistry
Auguste and Louis Lumiere and the Rise of Motion Pictures
Charles Babbage and the Story of the First Computer
Charles Darwin and the Origin of the Species
Dmitri Mendeleyev and the Periodic Table
Florence Nightingale and the Advancement of Nursing
Friedrich Miescher and the Story of Nucleic Acid
George Eastman and the Story of Photographic Film
Gregor Mendel and the Discovery of the Gene
Guglielmo Marconi and the Story of Radio Waves
Henry Bessemer: Making Steel from Iron
Henry Cavendish and the Discovery of Hydrogen
J. J. Thomson and the Discovery of Electrons
James Watt and the Steam Engine
John Dalton and the Atomic Theory
Joseph Lister and the Story of Antiseptics
Joseph Priestley and the Discovery of Oxygen
Karl Benz and the Single Cylinder Engine
Louis Daguerre and the Story of the Daguerreotype
Louis Pasteur: Fighter Against Contagious Disease
Michael Faraday and the Discovery of Electromagnetism
Pierre and Marie Curie and the Discovery of Radium
Robert Koch and the Study of Anthrax
Samuel Morse and the Story of the Electric Telegraph
Thomas Edison: Great Inventor

Visit us on the web: www.mitchelllane.com
Comments? email us: mitchelllane@mitchelllane.com

Uncharted, Unexplored, and Unexplained
Scientific Advancements of the 19th Century

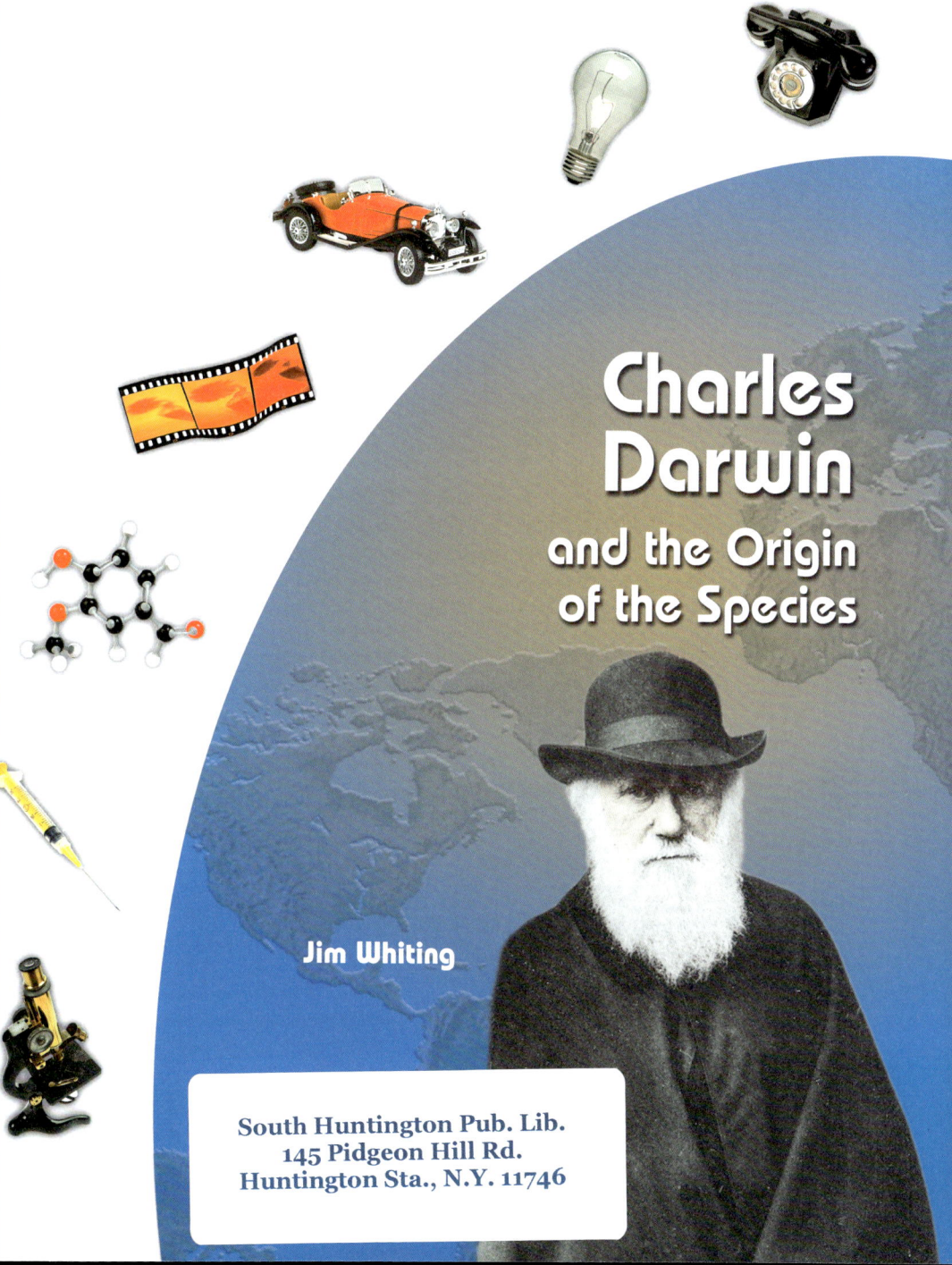

Charles Darwin
and the Origin of the Species

Jim Whiting

South Huntington Pub. Lib.
145 Pidgeon Hill Rd.
Huntington Sta., N.Y. 11746

Uncharted, Unexplored, and Unexplained
Scientific Advancements of the 19th Century

Copyright © 2006 by Mitchell Lane Publishers, Inc. All rights reserved. No part of this book may be reproduced without written permission from the publisher. Printed and bound in the United States of America.

Printing   2   3   4   5   6   7   8

Library of Congress Cataloging-in-Publication Data
Whiting, Jim, 1943–
  Charles Darwin and the origin of the species / by Jim Whiting.
    p. cm. — (Uncharted, unexplored, and unexplained)
  Includes bibliographical references and index.
  ISBN 1-58415-364-4 (library bound)
  1. Darwin, Charles, 1809–1882—Juvenile literature. 2. Naturalists—England—Biography—Juvenile literature. I. Title. II. Series.
QH31.D2W496 2005
576.8'2092—dc22
                                                                                            2005025421

ISBN-13: 9781584153641

ABOUT THE AUTHOR: Jim Whiting has been a remarkably versatile and accomplished journalist, writer, editor and photographer for more than 30 years. A voracious reader since early childhood, Mr. Whiting has written and edited about 200 non-fiction children's books. His subjects range from authors to zoologists and include contemporary pop icons and classical musicians, saints and scientists, emperors and explorers. Representative titles include *The Life and Times of Franz Liszt*, *The Life and Times of Julius Caesar*, *Charles Schulz*, *James Watt and the Steam Engine*, and *Juan Ponce de Leon*.
   Other career highlights are a lengthy stint publishing *Northwest Runner*, the first piece of original fiction to appear in *Runners World* magazine, hundreds of descriptions and venue photographs for *America Online*, e-commerce product writing, sports editor for the *Bainbridge Island Review*, light verse in a number of magazines and acting as the official photographer for the *Antarctica Marathon*.
   He lives in Washington state with his wife and two teenage sons.

PHOTO CREDITS: Cover, pp. 1, 3, 40—British Library; pp. 6, 12, 17, 18, 34, 36—Library of Congress; p. 22—Sharon Beck; p. 28—M. H. Museum; pp. 31, 33—Jamie Kondrchek; p. 39—Marxist Documents.

PUBLISHER'S NOTE: This story is based on the author's extensive research, which he believes to be accurate. Documentation of such research is contained on page 47.
   The internet sites referenced herein were active as of the publication date. Due to the fleeting nature of some web sites, we cannot guarantee they will all be active when you are reading this book.

PLB4

Uncharted, Unexplored, and Unexplained
Scientific Advancements of the 19th Century

Charles Darwin
and the Origin of the Species

Chapter 1	Who's Your Grand(Daddy)?	7
	FYInfo*: The Scopes Monkey Trial	11
Chapter 2	A Child of Privilege	13
	FYInfo: The Development of Anesthesia	21
Chapter 3	Sailing Around the World	23
	FYInfo: Robert FitzRoy	27
Chapter 4	The Book That Rocked the World	29
	FYInfo: Age of the Earth	35
Chapter 5	Fame and Final Years	37
	FYInfo: Other Theories	42

*For Your Information

Chronology	43
Selected Works	43
Timeline of Discovery	44
Chapter Notes	45–46
Glossary	46
For Further Reading	47
Works Consulted	47
On the Internet	47
Index	48

Bishop Samuel Wilberforce attacked Charles Darwin soon after his controversial book, *On the Origin of Species*, was published. Born in 1805, he was jokingly referred to as "Soapy Sam." A little girl once asked him about his nickname. He replied that he always came out clean when he got into hot water. He died in 1873.

Uncharted, Unexplored, and Unexplained

Scientific Advancements of the 19th Century

1

Who's Your Grand(Daddy)?

Bishop Samuel Wilberforce was not a happy man. "Soapy Sam" (as some people called him behind his back) was upset when a book entitled *On the Origin of Species by Means of Natural Selection* was published in 1859. Written by Charles Darwin, the book proposed a new theory: the theory of evolution. This theory stood in opposition to everything that Wilberforce believed. It especially challenged the biblical explanation that he and all other human beings were directly descended from Adam and Eve, whom God created in a contemporary human form.

A simplified and not very accurate version of the theory was circulated. Many of Wilberforce's fellow Englishmen were led to believe that Darwin was proposing something he was not. They thought he was saying that human beings were the direct descendents of monkeys and apes. Cartoonists were having a lot of fun with this idea. They drew illustrations that showed Darwin's distinctive head and facial features on the body of an ape.

The bishop didn't see any humor in the situation. He was convinced that, because the book threatened so many traditional beliefs, Darwin was the most dangerous man in England. Ironically, Wilberforce's father had been a good friend of both of Darwin's grandparents. For the bishop, those past

Chapter 1

Who's Your (Grand)Daddy?

friendships were not as important as what he thought was at stake. He intended to destroy Darwin's theory and strike down his growing influence.

On the last day of June in 1860, Wilberforce felt confident that he was in a good position to accomplish this task. He was the featured speaker at the annual meeting of the British Association for the Advancement of Science, and he was probably the most famous and most powerful clergyman in England. In addition to his prestige, he had a reputation as an excellent and forceful public speaker.

Wilberforce wasn't alone in opposing Darwin's theory. Other famous scientists and clergymen shared his opinion. Darwin had many supporters as well.

Because of the controversy, Darwin's theory was the hottest topic in the country. Hundreds of people had packed the hall in Oxford, England, where the annual meeting was being held. Darwin wasn't among them. He had hoped to attend, but he was suffering from ill health. However, two of his friends—Thomas Huxley and Joseph Hooker—were there. Both men were well-known scientists and fully supported Darwin.

Huxley and Hooker had good reason to be concerned as they listened to Wilberforce. The bishop used his skills to good advantage. As he neared the end of his speech, he had apparently convinced most of the audience that Darwin was both unreligious and unscientific.

Then he made a mistake. He turned to Huxley and sarcastically asked him if he claimed descent from the apes on his grandmother's or his grandfather's side of the family.

Huxley muttered, "The Lord hath delivered him into mine hands."[1] His response to Wilberforce's question was that if he had to choose between being descended from an ape or from a person who used his high position to stand in the way of scientific inquiry and ridicule people who only sought the truth, he would choose the ape.

The remark caused an uproar. People began yelling. At least one woman in the audience fainted. When the crowd calmed down, a few more people

Charles Darwin and the Origin of the Species

were allowed to speak. Finally the meeting ended. Darwin's allies claimed that they had overcome their opponents. Wilberforce's supporters came to the same conclusion.

In many cases, scientific theories make headlines when they are first announced, then gradually fade from the consciousness of most people. That has not been the case with Charles Darwin and the theory of evolution.

One of the most famous episodes occurred in 1925. The so-called Scopes Monkey Trial gained the same sort of headlines that we associate with the 2005 Michael Jackson trial and similar other high-profile court cases.

In recent years, the theory has frequently grabbed front-page coverage.

In 1999, two unhappy students murdered 13 people and wounded 21 more at Columbine High School in Colorado. In response, Congressman Tom DeLay of Texas tried to link the shootings to the teaching of evolution. "Our school systems teach the children that they are nothing but glorified apes who are evolutionized out of some primordial soup,"[2] he said.

Nature writer David Quammen notes that according to a 2001 Gallup Poll, "No less than 45 percent of responding American adults agreed that 'God created human beings pretty much in their present form at one time within the last 10,000 years or so.' . . . Still fewer Americans, only 12 percent, believed that humans evolved from other life-forms without any involvement of a god."[3]

That same year, a similar survey conducted by the National Science Foundation revealed that only 53 percent of Americans agreed with the statement, "Human beings, as we know them, developed from earlier species of animals."[4] It seemed apparent that in the United States, there was still a great deal of resistance to Darwin's theory. In fact, that 2001 survey was the first time that the statement had even received more than 50 percent agreement. It seemed apparent that there was still a great deal of opposition to Darwin's theory in the United States.

One example of this resistance surfaced the following year. The school board of Cobb County, Georgia, ordered stickers to be placed on a high

Chapter 1   **Who's Your (Grand)Daddy?**

school biology textbook. These stickers read: "This textbook contains material on evolution. Evolution is a theory, not a fact, regarding the origin of living things. This material should be approached with an open mind, studied carefully, and critically considered."[5]

Many people who disagree with Darwin's theory oppose it on religious grounds. So it is ironic that the textbook's author, Ken Miller, believes very deeply in the Roman Catholic faith. "I attend Mass every Sunday morning," he said, "and I'm tired of being called an atheist."[6] Miller had some satisfaction early in 2005 when a federal judge ordered the stickers to be removed.

In 2004, Pennsylvania's Dover Area School District voted to include the theory of intelligent design* in the ninth-grade science curriculum. It was probably the first such requirement in the country. Several parents, supported by the American Civil Liberties Union, protested. They maintained that "intelligent design" was religiously based and therefore violated the constitutional separation of church and state.

In 2005, an IMAX film entitled *Volcanoes of the Deep Sea* was withdrawn from theaters in several Southern states. The film contains references to evolution, connecting humans and microbes.

"We've got to pick a film that's going to sell in our area. If it's not going to sell, we're not going to take it," said the director of a Charleston, South Carolina, IMAX theater. "Many people here believe in creationism*, not evolution."[7]

It is likely that stories such as these will continue to receive prominent media coverage in the years to come.

*See page 42 for more on these theories.

The Scopes Monkey Trial

FYInfo

In February 1925, the Tennessee legislature made it illegal "to teach any theory that denies the story of divine creation as taught by the Bible and to teach instead that man was descended from a lower order of animals."[8] The American Civil Liberties Union immediately ran newspaper ads offering free legal services to anyone who taught the theory of evolution in Tennessee.

A group of businessmen in the small town of Dayton, Tennessee, wanted to generate publicity for their town. They asked John T. Scopes, a 24-year-old part-time high school science teacher and football coach, if he had taught evolution. Scopes wasn't sure. The textbook he used while filling in for the regular biology teacher did mention evolution, so Scopes said that he must have. He agreed to go on trial.

The prosecutors were two brothers who were good friends with Scopes. Three-time presidential candidate William Jennings Bryan, a religious fundamentalist, offered to help them. Clarence Darrow, perhaps the country's most famous trial lawyer, defended Scopes. The case became a media sensation. Billed as a "showdown" between religion and science, it was nicknamed the "monkey trial." Monkeys were the symbol of evolution for many people. Newspapers from all over the country sent reporters. Dozens of radio stations provided live coverage.

A carnival atmosphere prevailed in Dayton. Children sold lemonade in the streets. Banners flew everywhere. The town imported scores of monkeys. One was dressed in a three-piece suit and expensive shoes. When the trial opened on July 10, 1925, the spectators packed the courtroom, shoulder to shoulder.

The highlight came several days later when Bryan took the witness stand. Darrow questioned him closely about his religious beliefs. The exchange had nothing to with the actual case. The judge ordered the testimony removed from the record. By this point, Scopes had become almost forgotten. His main activity was filling in for an ill reporter and writing newspaper stories about his own trial.

The Scopes Monkey Trial

No one doubted the trial's outcome. Scopes was found guilty and was fined $100. Both sides claimed victory in the larger battle of religion vs. science.

Scopes's conviction was overturned on a technicality the following year. By then, he had left Dayton and the teaching profession.

11

Erasmus Darwin had a great deal of influence on his younger brother Charles. Born in 1804, Erasmus was about to start a medical career in 1829. But his father, Robert (a wealthy and famous physician), decided that the strain would be too great. He provided Erasmus with enough money for a comfortable living. Erasmus died in 1881 without ever having a career or a wife.

Uncharted, Unexplored, and Unexplained

Scientific Advancements of the 19th Century

2

A Child of Privilege

Charles Robert Darwin was born on February 12, 1809, in the town of Shrewsbury, England. (By coincidence, the future U.S. President Abraham Lincoln was born on the same day.) His father, Robert Darwin, was a wealthy physician. His mother was Susannah Wedgwood Darwin. Charles was the fifth of six children. He had three older sisters—Marianne, Caroline, and Susan—and an older brother, Erasmus. Another sister, Catherine, was born the year after Charles.

Both of Charles's grandfathers were among the most famous men in England. Erasmus Darwin was a successful doctor who had been offered the position of Royal Physician to King George III. He turned it down because he didn't want to leave his comfortable home and move to London. Josiah Wedgwood, his other grandfather, had perfected a way of mass-producing some of the world's finest china. He and Erasmus Darwin were very close friends. The friendship extended to their families. Robert Darwin and Susannah Wedgwood came to an "understanding" while they were still teenagers. They would get married when Robert became established in his medical practice.

Their wedding came in 1796, a year after Susannah's father had died. Josiah Wedgwood left his daughter enough money to purchase land and build a house for the family she and Robert expected to have.

Chapter 2

A Child of Privilege

Robert proved to be an outstanding physician. Although he was sensitive to the needs and concerns of his patients, some people found him to be intimidating. He had a forceful personality and was exceptionally large, eventually weighing well over 300 pounds.

Charles's first few years were happy and carefree. While his mother was often in ill health, his sisters loved taking care of him. There were cousins to play with. He had plenty of food to eat and plenty of places on the family property to play. He even had his own special seat in one of the largest trees.

He developed an enduring love of the natural world. "I tried to make out the names of plants, and collected all sorts of things, shells, seals, franks, coins, and minerals," he wrote. "The passion for collecting, which leads a man to be a systematic naturalist . . . was very strong in me."[1]

He also enjoyed harmless pranks. "As a little boy, I was much given to inventing deliberate falsehoods," he recalled, "and this was always done for the sake of causing excitement."[2]

Tragedy struck in 1817 when Susannah died. Many people at that time were not accustomed to show emotion. They kept their feelings bottled up. Robert's main release was his work. Another way he covered his grief was by constantly talking. Sometimes his children didn't want to be around him because he talked so much.

Charles's older sisters became his primary caregivers. While he appreciated what they did for him, sometimes he just wanted to get away from them. One way to escape was to spend time with the man who took care of the extensive gardens. Another was to fish in the nearby river. Charles also liked to go for long walks by himself.

When he was 10, he joined his brother at Shrewsbury School. They both lived at the school, even though it was only a mile from their home. Erasmus, 14, was content to stay there all the time. Not Charles. Frequently he would run home to spend part of the afternoon with his sisters. He calculated how much time he would need to run back before he'd be declared late.

Charles Darwin and the Origin of the Species

The school was very traditional. It emphasized subjects such as Latin and Greek. Charles, bored, did only enough schoolwork to pass. He was much more interested in subjects that the school didn't offer, such as studies of the natural world. He was fascinated by bugs and birds.

He also became interested in outdoor sports, especially shooting. He wrote later, "I do not believe that anyone could have shown more zeal for the most holy cause than I did for shooting birds. How well I remember killing my first snipe, and my excitement was so great that I had much difficulty in reloading my gun from the trembling of my hands."[3]

Charles hadn't yet realized that he was wealthy enough to spend his whole life doing things such as hunting birds and small animals. His father didn't encourage such activities. He wanted Charles to be something more than an idle rich man. Robert had been busy and productive for his entire life. He told Charles, "You care for nothing but shooting, dogs, and rat-catching; and you will be a disgrace to yourself and all your family."[4]

To help Charles find a more useful pursuit, Robert occasionally took his son when he went to see patients. Sometimes he even let Charles help care for them. Robert believed that Charles would make a fine physician. Erasmus was already at the University of Edinburgh in Scotland, completing his medical studies. Robert decided that Charles would join him there. It would remove the boy from the temptations of an idle sporting life and put him under the influence of his steady older brother.

Financially, Charles was completely dependent on his father. He had to do what Robert wanted. So in the fall of 1825, he went to Edinburgh, which was far larger than any other place he had lived. He enjoyed being with his brother. He also enjoyed the excitement of living in such a big city. But it didn't take him long to realize that he couldn't follow his father and become a doctor. He hated the class lectures. To him, they were dry and boring. Far worse was watching two operations. One was performed on a young child. At that time, there was no anesthesia. The child screamed from the pain. Charles was horrified by what he saw.

Soon he began to neglect his official studies. There were plenty of other things to fill up his time. He read books that interested him. He joined a

Chapter 2
A Child of Privilege

student society that discussed natural science. He went out with fishermen to study marine life. He learned how to stuff animals.

Eventually his father realized that his son would never be a physician. While he was disappointed, Robert would not force Charles to follow in his footsteps. But he would force him to choose another career. The options were very limited. Well-to-do Englishmen were not expected to work with their hands. Charles wouldn't consider joining the army or navy or becoming a lawyer. The only other alternative was to become a minister.

Though Charles's religious beliefs weren't very strong, the life of a country clergyman had some advantages. Aided by his father's wealth, he could live comfortably. He would have time to study the natural world that he so dearly loved. He could even take up shooting again.

Early in 1828, Charles began attending Cambridge University. He later commented, "During the three years which I spent at Cambridge my time was wasted, as far as the academical studies were concerned, as completely as at Edinburgh and at school."[5]

It didn't really matter. Though today Cambridge is one of the most highly regarded universities in the world, at that time the school didn't demand much of its students. Charles thoroughly enjoyed himself. He often went horseback riding. He played cards and had an active social life. He spent a great deal of time in the fields with his shotgun. He developed an appreciation for music and often listened to singing groups.

His interest in the natural world also continued. "No pursuit at Cambridge was followed with nearly so much eagerness or gave me so much pleasure as collecting beetles,"[6] he wrote. Once he found two rare beetles. He put one in each hand. Suddenly he saw a third. In his eagerness, he popped one he was holding into his mouth. The unhappy beetle squirted a harsh liquid onto his tongue. Charles spit it out and it ran away. He was so distracted that he also lost the one he had tried to grab.

Probably the most important thing that happened to Charles at Cambridge was meeting John Stevens Henslow, a botany professor. Henslow, who was also an ordained minister, was very impressed with

Charles Darwin and the Origin of the Species

Charles. The two men went on long walks together. Henslow often invited Charles to dinner, where he introduced him to other eminent scientists.

During his last months at Cambridge in 1831, Charles read Alexander von Humboldt's *Personal Narrative*, an account of the famous explorer's five-year expedition to South America. It made a great impression on him. He especially wanted to take a trip to the Atlantic Ocean island of Tenerife, where Humboldt had spent considerable time. Charles began making plans for the journey. To his dismay, he learned that he was too late to make the trip that year.

Instead, he went on a walking tour of Wales with geology professor Adam Sedgwick. It was Charles's introduction to geology, a subject that would soon become one of his most important areas of knowledge.

When he got home, he found a letter from Henslow. The few sheets of paper would change the course of scientific history.

Born in 1785, Adam Sedgwick became a geology professor at Cambridge University in 1818. He was a very active researcher. His efforts greatly enlarged the geology collection at the university. He was especially well known as an excellent lecturer. He remained active until just before his death in 1873.

Chapter 2   A Child of Privilege

Henslow began, "I have been asked . . . to recommend a naturalist as companion to Capt Fitz-Roy employed by Government to survey the southern extremity of America."[7] The "Capt Fitz-Roy" was Robert FitzRoy, the 26-year-old captain of HMS *Beagle*, a small ship that had already done over a year of survey work in the same area under his command.

FitzRoy was of noble birth. Because of the social system that existed at the time, the captain could not be close friends with anyone in the crew. To while away the lonely hours of a cruise that was anticipated to take at least two years, he needed another gentleman to accompany him. Not just any gentleman—it needed to be one who could add to the scientific objectives of the voyage, and one with plenty of time on his hands. Those requirements reduced the list of possible candidates to just a few men.

Henslow wasn't concerned that Darwin wasn't a professional scientist. "I consider you to be the best qualified person I know of . . . I state this not on the supposition of your being a finished Naturalist, but as amply qualified for collecting, observing, and noting anything worthy to be noted in Natural History. . . . Don't put on any modest doubts or fears about your

Robert Fitzroy was appointed captain of the Beagle when he was only 23. He led a successful naval career that lasted for more than 30 years. He also served as governor of New Zealand and is credited with being the first weather forecaster.

Charles Darwin and the Origin of the Species

qualifications for I assure you I think you are the very man they are in search of,"[8] he continued in the letter.

Darwin was overjoyed at the invitation. His father wasn't. Charles was an adult and didn't need his father's permission to go, but he did need his father's financial support. Charles was expected to pay his own way. After investing so much money in Charles's education, Robert wanted to see his son settle down. He thought that the voyage was the height of folly. It would allow Charles to put off his career even longer.

Firmly, Robert said no. Charles was bitterly disappointed, but he had to abide by his father's decision. Then, unexpectedly, Robert gave Charles an escape clause. If Charles could find a man of common sense who thought that he should go on the voyage, Robert would give his consent.

Charles knew just the man: his uncle, Josiah Wedgwood. He wrote down his father's objections and presented the list to "Uncle Jos."

1. Disreputable to my character as a Clergyman thereafter
2. A wild scheme
3. That they must have offered to many others before me, the place of Naturalist
4. And from its not being accepted there must be some serious objection to the vessel or expedition
5. That I should never settle down to a steady life hereafter
6. That my accommodation would be most uncomfortable
7. That you consider it as again changing my profession
8. That it would be a useless undertaking[9]

Josiah came through. He drafted a letter that addressed each of the eight objections that Robert Darwin had raised, then went with Charles to meet face to face with his father. It worked. Robert gave his consent.

Darwin soon headed for London to meet FitzRoy. While his only comment about the meeting was that "all was soon arranged,"[10] Darwin must have felt as if he had just hit the jackpot. He was even more excited when he learned that the first port of call would be Tenerife.

Chapter 2 — A Child of Privilege

Darwin later discovered that he nearly wasn't selected to go. During the voyage, when he and FitzRoy had become very close, he learned: "I had run a very narrow risk of being rejected, on account of the shape of my nose. He . . . was convinced that he could judge a man's character by the outline of his features; and he doubted whether anyone with my nose could possess sufficient energy and determination for the voyage."[11]

As things turned out, Darwin had more than enough energy and determination for the task. FitzRoy was a man with very deep-seated and rigid religious beliefs. He had focused on the wrong organ. Darwin's brain would eventually upset the foundations of everything that FitzRoy believed in.

The next step was a visit with FitzRoy to the *Beagle*. Darwin didn't record his reaction, but the sight of his home for at least two years to come must have been a shock. The ship was the length of a basketball court and nowhere near as wide. Yet more than seventy people would soon be aboard, along with the ship's 10 guns, food and supplies for several months at a time, and all their surveying and collecting equipment.

Darwin was given the largest cabin on the vessel. It measured 11 feet by 10 feet, and the ceiling was only 5 feet high. It wasn't Darwin's alone. The ship's chart table took up a lot of space. It had to because the main purpose of the voyage was to return with accurate charts. The young man who had spent most of his life sleeping in soft beds would now be sleeping in a hammock. It didn't help that his height was about six feet, extremely tall for that era.

Darwin spent several weeks saying good-bye to all his friends and relatives. He spent a few weeks in London, taking crash courses from experts in various fields. He needed to learn how to preserve the hundreds of specimens he anticipated collecting. He needed to purchase equipment such as microscopes, geological hammers, heavy boots, and more.

With little fanfare, the *Beagle* stood out to sea on the morning of December 27, 1831. No one aboard could know that it would become one of the most famous sea voyages of all time.

The Development of Anesthesia

FYInfo

Charles Darwin wasn't the only person to be horrified when watching people undergo surgery. For the patients, it was very painful. Sometimes they were given drugs to dull the pain. Others got drunk. Wounded soldiers were given bullets to clench between their teeth as their arms or legs were cut off with a surgical saw. This practice is the origin of the phrase "bite the bullet" for facing up to something very unpleasant.

Humphry Davy

In 1799, British scientist Humphry Davy discovered that nitrous oxide produced a fit of uncontrollable laughter (earning it the nickname "laughing gas,") followed by a brief period of unconsciousness. Hardly anyone paid attention.

Very little was done to relieve the suffering of patients until 1842, when Dr. Crawford Long used ether during minor surgery. He didn't publish his results until 1849. In 1844, a dentist named Horace Wells asked a student to remove one of Wells's teeth while he was under the influence of laughing gas. Wells felt no pain, but a public demonstration of the procedure failed.

The big breakthrough came on September 30, 1846. William Morton, a Boston dentist, used ether on a patient. The procedure was so successful that on October 16 Dr. John Charles Warren, one of the country's most respected physicians, used ether when he removed a small tumor on a patient's neck. The news of his success quickly spread.

Surprisingly, not everyone welcomed this discovery. William Atkinson, a prominent dentist, said, "I think anesthesia is of the devil, and I cannot give my sanction [approval]. I wish there were no such thing as anesthesia! I do not think men should be prevented from passing through what God intended them to endure."[12] Some military doctors didn't want to use it because they thought it was "unmanly."

English Queen Victoria gave a huge boost to anesthesia when she used it in 1853 during the birth of one of her children. Today it is used in medical and dental procedures that range from filling teeth to major operations that last for many hours. Veterinarians even use it to treat pets.

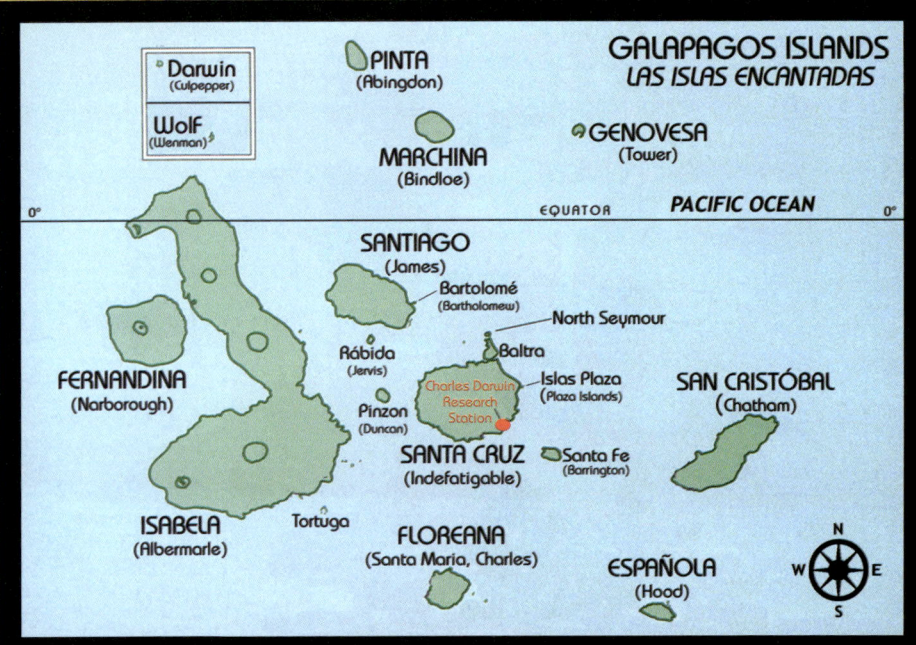

Charles Darwin is noted for his observations in the Galapagos Islands. He saw a wide variety of unusual animals. Even today visitors can experience much the same conditions as Darwin. The Charles Darwin Research Station honors his memory.

Uncharted, Unexplored, and Unexplained
Scientific Advancements of the 19th Century

3

Sailing Around the World

As soon as the *Beagle* cleared Plymouth harbor, Darwin realized he had the unfortunate tendency to become seasick. He tried to console himself with thoughts of going ashore at Tenerife. When the ship arrived there a week and a half later, he was very disappointed. Because of a cholera epidemic in England, all English ships were required to wait at anchor for nearly two weeks before anyone could go ashore. FitzRoy, who saw no reason for delay, hoisted the anchor and sailed away.

Darwin spent a great deal of time reading in his cabin. His favorite book was *Principles of Geology*, a controversial new work by Charles Lyell. Lyell challenged the prevailing belief that God occasionally would unleash tremendous forces against the earth. Known as catastrophism, the belief tried to account for why some species would suddenly disappear and others make their first appearance, and why the land would sometimes change its shape.

Lyell suggested that geological changes occurred very slowly over long periods of time. There were no great upheavals. His belief was called uniformitarianism.

Three weeks after leaving England, the ship anchored at the Cape Verde Islands. Darwin happily went ashore for a nearly three-week stay. To his amazement, he found a layer of seashells and coral 30 feet above sea level.

Chapter 3   Sailing Around the World

The only explanation he could think of was that the area had once been under water and had slowly risen upward. It seemed to offer evidence for Lyell's theory. It would be far from the last.

When the ship arrived at the coast of Brazil, Darwin believed that he had entered a sort of paradise. Everything fascinated him—the rain forest, the miles of perfect beaches, and especially the porcupine fish. When in danger, the creature puffed itself up and became very spiky. Even so, sometimes a shark would swallow it. The fish would remain alive. Occasionally one would eat its way through the shark's stomach and make its escape.

Several hundred miles farther south, a group of gauchos, or cowboys, took him to a place littered with the remains of dead animals. Many were far larger than any of the animals that currently lived in the area. Darwin began wondering about these animals. What had they looked like, and how had they died? Just as important, how long ago had they lived?

He made several other shore excursions, collecting many specimens of plant and animal life. To keep from being overwhelmed in the ship's tight quarters, he began sending them back to Henslow. He had no idea if anyone would be interested in them. He also included letters describing what he had seen. Henslow arranged for the letters to be read at meetings of English scientific societies.

In mid-December, the *Beagle* arrived at Tierra del Fuego at the tip of South America. The name means "land of fire," but even at what was the beginning of summer in the Southern Hemisphere, it was bleak, desolate, frequently wet, and always cold. The harsh conditions had reportedly driven the *Beagle*'s previous captain, Pringle Stokes, to commit suicide.

FitzRoy had a special interest in the region. After taking over for Stokes and continuing the *Beagle*'s survey work, he had taken three Fuegians aboard and brought them back to England. They became "civilized" and accustomed to wearing English clothing. Now he wanted to establish a Christian mission in Tierra del Fuego under the direction of Richard Matthews, a young clergyman. The three Fuegians would help Matthews.

Charles Darwin and the Origin of the Species

Soon after dropping them off, FitzRoy learned that Matthews's life was in danger. The missionary and the three Fuegians returned to the *Beagle*.

In March, the crew began surveying the Malvinas Islands (now known as the Falklands), about 200 miles to the east. A few weeks later they returned to Argentina. Darwin went ashore and continued his collecting. He also took several long, adventurous horseback rides.

The *Beagle* headed back for Tierra del Fuego in December 1833. Darwin had already been gone for the two years that the voyage had originally been planned for. Yet there was seemingly no end in sight. He didn't care. He was seeing so many things and enjoying himself so much (apart from his frequent seasickness) that he was in no hurry to return home.

Once again, Matthews was threatened when he went ashore and tried to set up his mission. He came back to the ship, leaving the three Fuegians behind in their native land. FitzRoy was upset by the failure of his plan.

The *Beagle* continued her voyage, working her way through what would become known as the Beagle Channel, then the Strait of Magellan, and finally, in June 1834, emerging on the west coast of South America.

In July, the *Beagle* anchored in Valparaiso, Chile's main port. For Darwin, the city was a welcome change from the bleakness of Tierra del Fuego. Equally welcome was the offer of shoreside accommodations from Richard Corfield, a boyhood friend. Darwin explored the Andes, the massive mountain range that rises to nearly 23,000 feet at the highest point.

On September 21, Darwin confided in his journal, "During the day I felt very unwell."[1] This was one of the first signs of a mysterious illness that would plague him for the rest of his life. He was bedridden at Corfield's house for more than a month.

The following January he saw a volcanic eruption, and a month later experienced a violent earthquake. He observed that the land had risen several feet as a result of the quake. Coupled with his discovery of seashells embedded in hills hundreds of feet above the sea, he believed that he had further evidence for Lyell's theory. "It is hardly possible to doubt that this great elevation has been effected by successive small uprisings, such as

Chapter 3
Sailing Around the World

that which accompanied or caused the earthquake of this year, and likewise by an insensibly slow rise,"[2] he wrote. With enough time, he thought, this "insensibly slow rise" could even have produced the Andes themselves.

Now the *Beagle* was ready to return home. In September 1835, the ship stopped in the Galápagos Islands, 600 miles off the coast of Ecuador, to take on food and water. For Darwin, it would prove to be the most momentous month of the entire voyage.

The Galápagos are also known as *Las Islas Encantadas* (The Enchanted Islands). The wildlife there was strange and exotic. There were tortoises so huge that men would ride them for fun. There were large lizards known as iguanas.

To Darwin, it was also strange that the animals on each island were slightly different from similar animals on the other islands. The inhabitants explained to Darwin that they could tell which island a tortoise had come from by the shape of its shell.

Strong ocean currents and other factors isolated each island from the others. It seemed that each island's creatures had developed independently, in their own way.

Darwin was especially interested in the finches, small brown birds that most people didn't pay much attention to. Darwin did. He noticed that each island had a unique type of finch. The birds were primarily differentiated by the size and shape of their beaks. At first he didn't think much of what he had seen. Later, the different beaks would anchor a crucial part of his thinking.

The *Beagle* continued across the Pacific, making a number of stops at islands along the way. Then the ship rounded the southern tip of Africa and made her way north into the Atlantic Ocean. The leisurely pace allowed plenty of time for Darwin to begin thinking about everything he had seen.

On October 2, 1836, the *Beagle* sailed into Falmouth harbor, on the southern coast of England. Charles Darwin had returned home. He would never leave England again.

Robert FitzRoy

Robert FitzRoy was born in 1805 to one of England's wealthiest and most respected families. He began attending the Royal Naval College when he was just 12 and joined the Royal Navy two years later. He was promoted to lieutenant in 1824 and became captain of HMS Beagle—his first command—late in 1828. The ship was in Patagonia, at the tip of South America, doing survey work. He brought the ship home to England in 1830. The following year, he was ordered to go back to South America with the Beagle and continue the work he had begun. That was when he met Charles Darwin and undertook the voyage that would make both of them—and the Beagle—famous.

After returning, FitzRoy published his account of the voyage. He was elected to Parliament, then received an appointment as governor of New Zealand. He remained in the navy, eventually rising to the rank of vice admiral.

In 1859, he set up the first weather station to warn seamen of approaching storms. Soon afterward, the London Times began publishing his forecasts. Weather forecasting, then as now, was not an exact science. Operating without the technological advances that modern-day forecasters enjoy, FitzRoy did the best he could. But his inevitable mistakes doomed him. The paper discontinued his forecasts and fired him in 1864.

By then, he was fully aware of the impact of Charles Darwin's writings. He was horrified that the man he had selected as his traveling companion was undermining belief in the Bible, in which he believed very strongly. At the Oxford meeting in 1860, he had stood up and waved a Bible, shouting that it contained "the truth."

Robert FitzRoy's grave

Coming from a family with a long history of depression, FitzRoy suffered from the same illness. On the morning of April 30, 1865, he got up, kissed his daughter, went into his dressing room, and cut his throat with a razor.

His contemporaries recognized his accomplishments. "No naval officer ever did more for the practical benefit of navigation and commerce than he did,"[3] wrote Admiral George Henry Richards soon after FitzRoy's death.

He soon was nearly forgotten, known only for his contribution to Darwin's theory. In 2002, a large expanse of open ocean near Spain that he had originally named Finisterre ("end of the earth") in his weather reports was renamed sea area FitzRoy to honor him.

Charles Darwin was one of the most famous men in England when this image was created. His bald head and long white beard made him instantly recognizable. Some cartoonists made fun of him. They put his head on the body of a monkey.

Uncharted, Unexplored, and Unexplained
Scientific Advancements of the 19th Century

4
The Book That Rocked the World

After a long, grueling sea voyage, many people would want to spend a long time unwinding. Not Darwin.

"[The next] two years and three months were the most active ones which I ever spent, though I was occasionally unwell and so lost some time,"[1] he wrote.

First, of course, was returning home to see his family. Soon after that, he settled in London. The aimless young man who had boarded the *Beagle* five years earlier had vanished along the thousands of miles that the ship had covered. Darwin had found his purpose in life. He had a great deal to do. He wanted to publish the journal he had kept during the voyage. He needed to work on his specimens. Because of everything he had sent home, he had become a respected member of the scientific community. He made a number of appearances before scientific groups.

His most important activity began less than a year after his return. He started on a project that would end more than two decades later. Its influence would last far longer.

As he noted, "In July 1 [1837] I opened my first note-book for facts in relation to the *Origin of Species,* about which I had long reflected, and never ceased working on for the next twenty years."[2]

Chapter 4

The Book That Rocked the World

His mind was especially active during this period. "While on board the *Beagle* I was quite orthodox, and I remember being heartily laughed at by several of the officers (though themselves orthodox) for quoting the Bible as an unanswerable authority on some point of morality," he wrote. "But I had gradually come, by this time, to see that the Old Testament from its manifestly false history of the world . . . was no more to be trusted than the sacred books of the Hindoos [Hindus], or the beliefs of any barbarian."[3]

For Darwin's era, this statement was shocking enough. But he was just getting warmed up. In 1838, a key element of his thinking fell into place. He read Thomas Malthus's *Essay on the Principle of Population*. Malthus maintained that, given existing food supplies, too many people were being born to be able to survive and reproduce. There would be a struggle for existence, which only the strongest would win.

Darwin applied the same principle to animals. He had observed that within a given species, small differences, such as the variety of beaks among the Galápagos finches, often developed. These differences could offer an advantage in the struggle for survival. The sources of food on each of the Galápagos Islands were different. One island might have large hard seeds on which the finches could feed. Another might have insects. Cacti would be dominant on a third. As new finches hatched, some would have slight variations in their beaks that made them more efficient in gathering the type of food that was unique to their island. This efficiency allowed more of them to survive. The survivors in turn would produce even more offspring with this particular beak. Over a long period of time, they would become the only finches on that island. They would have become adapted to their environment.

Darwin named this process "natural selection." It became the cornerstone of his theory. It also became the cornerstone of the controversy that would erupt many years later. The traditional biblical view was that God created all the creatures the way they were. They couldn't change. Yet according to Darwin, they did change.

"The old argument of design in nature . . . fails, now that the law of natural selection has been discovered," he wrote. "We can no longer argue that, for example, the beautiful valve must have been made by an intelligent

Charles Darwin and the Origin of the Species

People usually don't pay much attention to finches. Darwin was no exception. It was only when he returned to England that he thought about slight differences in their beaks. Those differences provided a key to his theory of natural selection.

being, like the hinge of a door by man. . . . Everything in nature is the result of fixed laws."[4]

These fixed laws needed time to operate—a great deal of time. According to their reading of the Old Testament, many Christians believed that the earth was only a few thousand years old. Darwin figured that that would have been nowhere near enough time for natural selection to work. He was already thinking in terms of a much older Earth. The time factor was another point in his theory that would lead to controversy.

Darwin's mind wasn't entirely devoted to science. By this time he was nearly 30, past the age at which most men of his era got married. He wrote down a list of reasons for and against having a wife and family. After going back and forth for months, he came to a conclusion: He didn't want to spend the rest of his life by himself. "Picture to yourself a nice soft wife on a sofa with a good fire, and books and music perhaps. . . . Marry—Marry—Marry,"[5] he wrote.

While Darwin had disregarded his father's example in some ways, in matrimony it was a case of "like father, like son." His father had married a Wedgwood. So would he. Darwin proposed to his cousin Emma Wedgwood, whom he had known since they were children. They were wed on

Chapter 4
The Book That Rocked the World

January 29, 1839. There was no honeymoon because Darwin was too busy. By the end of the year, they had a son, William Erasmus. Fifteen months later, Anne Elizabeth was born.

At first the couple was very active socially. Soon Darwin found himself too easily fatigued to go out so often. It was another ominous sign that the disease that had plagued him in Chile was resurfacing.

In 1842, the family moved to Down House, a country estate in Kent County. It would remain Darwin's home for the rest of his life.

Two years later, he wrote a 230-page summary of his ideas. Soon he began writing about these ideas to his friends. He urged them to maintain secrecy. Darwin was all too aware of the harsh fate that frequently awaited scientists who proposed theories that conflicted with strongly held beliefs. He had to back up his claims with evidence. Putting the evidence in order would be a time-consuming process.

His difficulties were compounded because he didn't like controversy—and he was certain that his new theory would cause a great deal of controversy. He had already had a taste of what could happen. In 1839, he published what is commonly known as *A Naturalist's Voyage*. (Its original title was *Journal of Researches into the Geology and Natural History of the Various Countries visited by H.M.S. 'Beagle' under the Command of Capt. FitzRoy, R.N., from 1832 to 1836*.) Some people criticized the book. They believed that the land had not risen gradually, as he said it had. The shells he mentioned had been placed there during Noah's flood, they argued. Darwin knew that people would be even more upset if they heard the ideas that were starting to fill his notebooks.

As he continued putting his ideas in order, he often branched out into specific areas of research. For example, he worked for eight years on the study of barnacles. He published two books on his findings, in 1851 and 1854.

Then he began concentrating on his ideas about evolution. The friends who knew what he was doing urged him to make haste. Someone else might be working on the same ideas, they told him.

Charles Darwin and the Origin of the Species

Barnacles are similar to shrimp. They find a solid surface and attach themselves to it. They form a hard shell. Their life cycle is one to seven years.

Someone else was. Darwin received a profound shock on June 18, 1858. He read an essay and its accompanying letter from a young naturalist named Alfred Russel Wallace. Wallace had been working in the jungles of the Malay Peninsula. He too had read Malthus's essay. It helped him to arrive at many of the same conclusions that Darwin had. He wrote to ask for Darwin's help in getting his work published.

Darwin was dumbfounded. He felt that two decades of hard work could be swept away if Wallace's ideas appeared in print before his. Yet he was a very honest man. Wallace had confided in him. He knew that the essay deserved to be published, and that he—Darwin—should be the one to arrange for that to happen. He did have one advantage: his hundreds of pages of meticulously recorded examples. But the massive manuscript he was working on wasn't anywhere near ready for publication.

His friends urged Darwin to present both an outline of his work and Wallace's essay at a scientific meeting the following month. That would show that Darwin had come up with the idea first. The scientists at the meeting listened attentively, but there was no particular excitement.

It was obvious to Darwin that he had to publish his book, and publish it as soon as possible. The need for haste made him decide on a much shorter version, which he entitled *On the Origin of Species by Means of Natural*

Chapter 4

The Book That Rocked the World

Alfred Russel Wallace briefly ran the family surveying business. Then he spent four years in Brazil and eight years in southern Asia observing the natural world. His conclusions were almost identical to Darwin's.

Selection. Even though it was nearly 500 pages, he considered it as an "abstract," a summary of the far longer work that he had originally envisioned.

It nearly didn't make it. He was constantly ill during the months that it took him to finish writing the book. Then he sent a significant portion to his friend Joseph Hooker, asking for last-minute comments. Somehow the manuscript wound up in the same drawer in which Hooker's children kept their art supplies. They believed that it had been put there for them to practice on. So they cut, colored, and scribbled on most of the pages, ruining them. Hooker was horrified and embarrassed. Darwin wrote back that he still had the original with all the corrections that he had made. "Otherwise," he continued, "the loss would have killed me."[6]

The initial printing of 1,250 copies went on sale in bookstores on November 22, 1859. To Darwin's astonishment, every copy was purchased that same day. The same thing happened to a second press run of 3,000 copies a few weeks later. Further editions soon followed.

Although the sudden appearance of Wallace's essay came as a shock to Darwin, it may have worked out for the best. "Had I published on the scale in which I began to write in 1856, the book would have been four or five times as large as the *Origin,* and very few would have had the patience to read it,"[7] he later wrote.

People did read it. Charles Darwin was about to become one of the most famous—and controversial—figures in scientific history.

Age of the Earth

FYInfo

In the first half of the 17th century, Bishop James Ussher of Ireland calculated the day that the world began. He carefully read several sources, in particular the Book of Genesis, and noted how long the people it mentions lived. Adding up all the numbers, he concluded that God created the earth on Sunday, October 23, 4004 B.C. John Lightfoot soon added the exact time, 9:00 in the morning. According to Ussher, Adam and Eve were expelled from the Garden of Eden 18 days later—Monday, November 10— and Noah's Ark came to rest on Mount Ararat on Wednesday, May 5, 2348 B.C.

Ussher's reasoning was included in an edition of the Bible that was published in 1701. Soon it became almost as well established as the Bible's original contents. Today, some people believe that the date of 4004 B.C. is accurate.

French naturalist Georges Buffon was among the first to challenge Ussher's calculations. In 1749, he published a book that estimated the age of the earth at 80,000 years. He based his estimate on the amount of time that it took a heated iron ball to cool down.

Within a few decades, geology—the study of the earth and especially its rock formations—began to emerge as a new science. As the 19th century began, geologists routinely spoke of millions of years as the age of the earth. By Darwin's time, references to "hundreds of millions of years" were common.

In 1896, French scientist Henri Becquerel discovered radiation, the process by which minerals slowly give off subatomic particles. About 10 years later, American scientist Bertram Boltwood used radiation decay to determine that some rocks were more than 2 billion years old. Continued research has uncovered rocks on every continent that are estimated to have existed for about 3.5 billion years. As the U.S. Geological Survey Web Site points out, "These ancient rocks have been dated by a number of radiometric dating methods and the consistency of the results give scientists confidence that the ages are correct to within a few percent."[8]

Henri Becquerel

Other calculations have placed the age of the Solar System—and therefore the earth—at about 4.5 billion years.

Richard Owen was the most famous scientist to oppose Darwin's theory. He began his professional life as a physician. He became very interested in natural history. He studied fossils and made up the word "dinosaur" in 1842.

5

Fame and Final Years

It didn't take long for reactions to Darwin's theory to begin pouring in. Huxley, Hooker, and Lyell all supported Darwin. So did many other eminent scientists. Henslow did not. Neither did Adam Sedgwick, with whom Darwin had traveled in Wales.

The most savage attack came from Richard Owen, a respected paleontologist with the British Museum and acquaintance of Darwin's. Owen wrote a 45-page article opposing the book and accusing the author of spreading falsehoods. He operated behind the scenes at the famous Oxford debate, advising Wilberforce on what to say.

As often happens with scholarly work, many people misread Darwin's book. The most common error was saying that Darwin believed humans were directly descended from apes. Darwin never said that. In fact, he said almost nothing about the origin of human beings. Virtually his only comment on the subject in *The Origin of Species* was this: "In the future I see open fields for far more important researches. . . . Much light will be thrown on the origin of man and his history."[1]

Darwin himself helped throw some light on the subject in a later book, *The Descent of Man*, which was published in 1871. It included two important points.

Chapter 5
Fame and Final Years

One was that qualities people had thought belonged only to humans also appeared in animals. These qualities just weren't as well developed. They included traits such as long-term memory, having a sense of beauty, imitating the behavior of others, and the ability to learn. One example was a fish that kept smashing against a pane of glass in an aquarium. Several fish were on the other side of the pane. After three months, it learned it couldn't break through. It stopped trying. Darwin said that a monkey wouldn't have taken nearly as long, and a human would have given up almost immediately. The point was that all three types of beings learned from experience.

The other point was what he called sexual selection. It took two forms. One was when males competed directly against each other for the right to mate with a female. The other was when different males tried to impress a single female, and the female made the choice. In both cases, he believed, the stronger males would usually be selected. That would help to pass on traits more suitable for survival.

By then his basic theory had become much more accepted. *The Descent of Man* didn't inspire anywhere near the furor that *The Origin of Species* had generated.

In his personal life, Darwin was mostly happy. He and Emma eventually had ten children, seven of whom lived to adulthood. But his mysterious illness—to this day, no one is sure what it was—continued to plague him.

Part of his happiness was living long enough to see his theory of evolution survive its initial attacks and become generally accepted. He remained intellectually active almost until the time of his death. He published his final book, *The Formation of Vegetable Mould Through the Action of Worms,* in 1881. While it may seem curious that a man who had written one of the most momentous books in scientific history would spend his final years studying earthworms, famed nature writer Stephen Jay Gould thinks differently.

"This humble little creature putting solids through its body, millions of them over thousands of years, can do an immense amount of work and so can evolution," Gould says. "It is a brilliant summation [of Darwin's entire

Charles Darwin and the Origin of the Species

> **Stephen Jay Gould became a professor of evolutionary biology at Harvard University in 1967. He published many popular books and articles about science. He died in 2002.**

life's work] and it was true to his principle that it is not fatuous ideas that will change the world, but it is patient and humble understanding of how nature works."[2]

Darwin probably would have agreed with Gould's assessment. At the end of his autobiography, Darwin listed the personal qualities that had been the most important in his work: "love of science—unbounded patience in long reflecting over any subject—industry in observing and collecting facts—and a fair share of invention as well as of common-sense."[3]

Just after his earthworm book was published, Darwin's already fragile health began to falter. He had a series of heart problems. In midafternoon on April 19, 1882, he died peacefully in his home, with his wife of 43 years gently cradling his head.

While Bishop Wilberforce might have objected had he still been alive, Darwin was buried in Westminster Abbey—the center of the Anglican Church. Darwin had long since made his peace with church authorities. His theories had become so well supported that many clergymen accepted them. In fact, two members of the clergy were among his eight pallbearers. Even today, many denominations such as Roman Catholicism don't see any conflict between the theory of evolution and their faith.

As authors Julian Huxley and H.B.D. Kettlewell point out, "And so the two greatest scientists that England has produced came to lie side by side in the Abbey—[Sir Isaac] Newton [most famous for his discovery of the laws of

Chapter 5   Fame and Final Years

> Westminster Abbey in London is one of the most famous churches in the world. Construction began in about 1050. It is the scene of the coronation of English monarchs. Many famous English citizens are buried there.

gravity], who banished miracles from the physical world . . . and Darwin, who banished not only miracles but also creation and design from the world of life, robbed God of his role of creator of man, and man of his divine origin."[4]

In spite of its general acceptance, holes were found in Darwin's theory. One of the primary questions was how exactly were variations in a particular species introduced. While Darwin was finalizing his book, an obscure monk named Gregor Mendel was working on that very problem in a monastery in Brno, which is located in modern-day Czech Republic. Even though Mendel published his findings on heredity in 1866, it took more than three decades for them to come to the notice of the scientific community. Building on Mendel's foundation, further research unlocked the secrets of deoxyribonucleic acid (DNA), the basic building block of heredity.

40

Charles Darwin and the Origin of the Species

Since Mendel and others have helped to clarify Darwin's hypothesis, the fundamental elements of the theory of evolution—especially natural selection—have become widely accepted in most industrialized countries. However, a significant number of people in the United States have continued to oppose it.

Bill Allen, editor of *National Geographic* magazine, offers one way to look at the ongoing controversy. "Some of the confusion stems from the phrase the 'theory of evolution,' " he explains. "When scientists say 'theory,' they mean a statement based on observation or experimentation that explains facets of the observable world so well that it becomes accepted as fact. They do not mean an idea created out of thin air, nor do they mean an unsubstantiated belief."[5]

Still, many Americans are skeptical of the theory. After all, for about 1,400 years, people accepted Ptolemy's theory that the sun and stars traveled around the earth. His theory was supported by observation, and the mathematical equations he used to explain the theory worked. It wasn't until Copernicus put forth a new theory in 1543 that people began accepting the idea that the earth orbited the sun.

Skepticism over Darwin's theory seems likely to continue. Thousands of cars in the United States have an emblem of a large fish eating a smaller fish that contains the word *Darwin*. Because the fish is one of the symbols of Christianity, the emblem signifies that the Christian religion is greater than Darwin's ideas.

In spite of opposition to his theory, Charles Darwin remains one of the primary examples of a person who "followed his dream." Early in his life, he developed a love of the natural world and the creatures that inhabit it. He maintained this passion while he was growing up, even though his father wanted him to redirect his energy and settle down into a traditional career.

Then he was fortunate enough to be offered a position that would enable him to pursue his interests. As we might say today, he decided to "go for it." He went further than he could have possibly imagined. Charles Darwin became one of the most recognizable figures in the entire history of science.

FYInfo

Other Theories

There are two major theories that counter the Darwinian view of evolution. One is Creationism. *The other is* Intelligent Design.

Creationism *contains a number of variations, though all followers postulate the existence of God. Some believe that the earth is flat or that the earth is the center of the universe.* Young-Earth Creationists *believe that the sun is at center of the solar system, but maintain that the Bible is literally true: The earth is between 6,000 and 10,000 years old, life was created in six 24-hour days, and God flooded the entire planet after Noah built the Ark.*

Old-Earth Creationists *agree that evidence supports an ancient earth, but they believe that God created life.* Progressive Creationism *agrees with most theories of physical science but rejects evolutionary biology, maintaining that God created life on earth. According to* Gap Creationism, *there was a long gap after the first chapter and first verse of the Book of Genesis ("In the beginning God created the heaven and the earth") and the rest of the Creation story, allowing both a very ancient earth and that God created everything on the earth.* Day-Age Creationism *maintains that each "day" in the Bible actually stands for a much longer period of time.*

Because all forms of Creationism refer specifically to God, it is difficult to teach them in public schools. The U.S. Constitution forbids public schools from teaching the belief system of any organized religion as factual.

Intelligent Design *is a comparatively recent development. It says that life on Earth is too complicated to be explained by natural selection. Therefore, life must have been deliberately designed by some form of intelligence. Believers in ID don't say exactly what this "form of intelligence" is. As a result, they maintain that it can and should be taught in schools because it doesn't mention God.*

Other major religions such as Islam and Hinduism have their own versions of how the world came to be. Hundreds of other cultures also have creation myths. Many people believe the word myth means something that isn't true. As religion writer Mark Isaak points out, "A myth is simply a story which is (or has been) considered true and sacred by a group of people."[6]

Chronology

1809	Born February 12 in Shrewsbury, England
1817	Mother dies
1819	Enters Shrewsbury School as boarding student
1825	Enters Edinburgh University to study medicine
1828	Enters Cambridge University with the intention of becoming a clergyman
1831	Departs from England on the HMS *Beagle* on December 27
1835	Visits Galápagos Islands
1836	Returns to England
1839	Marries his cousin Emma Wedgwood; son William is born
1842	Moves from London to Down House in Kent
1848	Father dies
1856	Begins writing *On the Origin of Species by Means of Natural Selection*
1859	Publishes *On the Origin of Species*
1871	Publishes *The Descent of Man*
1882	Dies on April 19 and is buried in Westminster Abbey

Selected Works

1839	*A Naturalist's Voyage* (original title: *Journal of Researches into the Geology and Natural History of the Various Countries visited by H.M.S. 'Beagle' under the Command of Capt. FitzRoy, R.N., from 1832 to 1836*); and *Zoology of the Voyage of H.M.S. Beagle* (published 1839–1843 in five volumes by various authors, edited and superintended by Charles Darwin)
1842	*The Structure and Distribution of Coral Reefs*
1844	*Geological Observations of Volcanic Islands*
1846	*Geological Observations on South America*
1851	*A Monograph of the Sub-class Cirripedia, with Figures of all the Species. The Lepadidae; or, Pedunculated Cirripedes* (a book about barnacles)
1854	*A Monograph of the Sub-class Cirripedia, with Figures of all the Species. The Balanidae (or Sessile Cirripedes); the Verrucidae, etc.* (another book about barnacles)
1858	*On the Perpetuation of Varieties and Species by Natural Means of Selection*
1859	*On the Origin of Species by Means of Natural Selection, or the Preservation of Favoured Races in the Struggle for Life*
1862	*On the Various Contrivances by which British and Foreign Orchids Are fertilised by Insects*
1868	*Variation of Plants and Animals Under Domestication*
1871	*The Descent of Man, and Selection in Relation to Sex*
1872	*The Expression of Emotions in Man and Animals*
1875	*Movement and Habits of Climbing Plants*
1875	*Insectivorous Plants*
1876	*The Effects of Cross- and Self-Fertilisation in the Vegetable Kingdom*
1877	*The Different Forms of Flowers on Plants of the Same Species*
1880	*The Power of Movement in Plants*
1881	*The Formation of Vegetable Mould Through the Action of Worms*
1887	*Autobiography of Charles Darwin* (Edited by his son Francis Darwin)

Timeline of Discovery

1759	Josiah Wedgwood establishes his pottery company.
1764	Wolfgang Amadeus Mozart writes his first symphony at the age of eight.
1775	British inventor James Watt develops the first practical steam engine.
1783	The Peace of Versailles establishes the United States as an independent country.
1791	The Bill of Rights, the first 10 amendments to the U.S. Constitution, is ratified.
1804	Alexander von Humboldt completes five-year scientific journey to South America, Cuba, and Mexico.
1809	Louis Braille, who will invent a system that allows blind people to read, is born.
1815	Napoléon is defeated at the Battle of Waterloo and is exiled to the remote Atlantic island of St. Helena, which begins nearly a century of peace in Europe.
1831	Sir James Clark Ross determines the position of the magnetic North Pole, which becomes vital for navigation.
1836	Nearly 200 Texans die as Mexicans win the battle of the Alamo.
1842	English scientist Richard Owen invents the word *dinosaur*.
1848	The United States wins the Mexican-American War and gains all or part of California, Nevada, Utah, New Mexico, Arizona, Colorado, and Wyoming, as well as recognizing the right of Texas to exist.
1859	Digging on the Suez Canal begins; it is completed 10 years later, shortening the voyage between Europe and Asia by several thousand miles.
1865	U.S. President Abraham Lincoln is assassinated.
1883	British author Robert Louis Stevenson writes *Treasure Island*.
1896	Emma Darwin dies.
1905	Albert Einstein publishes an account of his special theory of relativity, changing the way people view the everyday world.
1922	William Jennings Bryan begins an anti-evolution crusade, and its impact is soon felt in neighboring Tennessee.
1925	High school teacher John T. Scopes is placed on trial in Tennessee for teaching Darwin's theory of evolution.
1927	Belgian priest Georges Lemaître formulates Big Bang theory of the origin of the universe, estimating it occurred between 10 billion and 20 billion years ago.
1944	American scientist Oswald Avery publishes a paper demonstrating that DNA is the means by which characteristics are passed from one generation to another.
1953	Scientists James Watson and Francis Crick announce the structure of DNA.
1972	In Africa, Richard Leakey and Glynn Isaac discover what they believe to be the skull of a primitive ancestor of humans and estimate its age to be 2.5 million years old.
2005	Several IMAX theaters in the southern United States refuse to show a film about volcanoes because it presents information on DNA as evidence to support the theory of evolution.

Chapter Notes

Chapter 1   Who's Your (Grand)Daddy?
1. Julian Huxley and H.B.D. Kettlewell, *Charles Darwin and His World* (New York: Viking Press, 1965), p. 78.
2. Evolution Revolution, http://www.pbs.org/wgbh/evolution/religion/revolution/1990.html.
3. David Quammen, "Was Darwin Wrong?" *National Geographic,* November 2004, p. 6.
4. Cornelia Dean, "Evolution Takes a Back Seat in U.S. Classes," *The New York Times,* February 1, 2005, http://www.theocracywatch.org/schools_evolution_back_seat_times_jan1_05.htm.
5. Froma Harrop, "Finding Common Ground Between God and Evolution," *Seattle Times,* January 25, 2005, http://seattletimes.nwsource.com/html/opinion/2002159485_harrop25.html.
6. Ibid.
7. Associated Press, "Evolution Reference Hurts Volcano Film," March 23, 2005, http://www.movielords.com/3-evolution-reference-hurts-volcano-film.html.
8. *An Introduction to the Scopes (Monkey) Trial,* http://www.law.umkc.edu/faculty/projects/ftrials/scopes/evolut.htm.

Chapter 2   A Child of Privilege
1. Charles Darwin, *The Autobiography of Charles Darwin,* edited by Nora Barlow (New York: W. W. Norton & Company, 1969), p. 23.
2. Ibid., pp. 22–23.
3. Cyril Aydon, *Charles Darwin* (New York: Carroll & Graf, 2002), p. 19.
4. Ibid., p. 21.
5. Darwin, p. 58.
6. Ibid., p. 62.
7. Aydon, p. 39.
8. John Bowlby, *Charles Darwin: A New Life* (New York: W. W. Norton, 1990), p. 109.
9. Ibid., p. 110.
10. Darwin, p. 72.
11. Ibid.
12. Collect Medical Antiques, "General Surgery & Amputation," http://www.collectmedicalantiques.com/amputation3.html.

Chapter 3   Sailing Around the World
1. Christopher Ralling (editor), *The Voyage of Charles Darwin* (New York: Mayflower Books, 1979), p. 119.
2. Ibid., p. 123.
3. Peter Nichols, *Evolution's Captain* (New York: HarperCollins, 2003), p. 327.

Chapter 4   The Book That Rocked the World
1. Charles Darwin, *The Autobiography of Charles Darwin,* edited by Nora Barlow (New York: W. W. Norton & Company, 1969), p. 82.
2. Ibid., p. 83.
3. Ibid.
4. Ibid., p. 87.
5. Julian Huxley and H.B.D. Kettlewell, *Charles Darwin and His World* (New York: Viking Press, 1965), p. 57.
6. Cyril Aydon, *Charles Darwin* (New York: Carroll & Graf, 2002), p. 207.
7. Darwin, p. 124.
8. USGS, "Age of the Earth," October 9, 1997, http://pubs.usgs.gov/gip/geotime/age.html.

Chapter Notes

Chapter 5 Fame and Final Years
1. Charles Darwin, *The Illustrated Origin of Species* (New York: Hill and Wang, 1979), p. 222.
2. Melvyn Bragg, *On Giants' Shoulders: Great Scientists and Their Discoveries* (New York: John Wiley & Sons, 1998), p. 184.
3. Charles Darwin, *The Autobiography of Charles Darwin*, edited by Nora Barlow (New York: W. W. Norton & Company, 1969), p. 145.
4. Julian Huxley and H.B.D. Kettlewell, *Charles Darwin and His World* (New York: Viking Press, 1965), p. 126.
5. Bill Allen, "From the Editor," *National Geographic*, November 2004, p. xvi.
6. Mark Isaak, "What Is Creationism?" May 30, 2000, http://www.talkorigins.org/faqs/wic.html.

Glossary

atheist (AY-thee-ust)—a person who doesn't believe in God or gods.

catastrophism (kuh-TASS-truh-fih-zum)—belief that Earth's geological features were created by a series of sudden and very powerful physical events.

cholera (KAH-luh-ruh)—a disease of the digestive system that causes severe diarrhea and in the past was often fatal.

creationism (kree-AY-shun-izm)—belief that the universe and everything in it was created directly by God.

ether (EE-thur)—a substance used to put people to sleep long enough that they can undergo surgery without feeling pain.

evolution (eh-vuh-LOO-shun)—changing slowly, via small steps, over a long period of time.

fatuous (FA-chew-us)—foolish, ridiculous.

forecasts (FOR-kasts)—predictions of upcoming events or conditions.

fundamentalist (fun-duh-MEN-tuh-list)—a person who emphasizes living by the literal truth of the Bible or other religious writings.

gauchos (GOW-chose)—the Argentinean equivalent of cowboys.

intelligent design (inn-TELL-uh-junt deh-ZYNE)—belief that life on Earth is so complicated that it can only have come about under the direction of some type of intelligent being.

nitrous oxide (NIE-truss AHK-side)—a colorless gas composed of nitrogen and oxygen that when inhaled produces laughter and brief periods of unconsciousness.

orthodox (OR-thuh-docks)—acting in accord with commonly accepted beliefs, especially religious beliefs.

paleontologist (PAY-lee-on-TAH-luh-jist)—a scientist who studies fossils to determine geologic history.

primordial (pry-MOR-dee-uhl)—belonging to the very beginning of a process.

snipe A small game bird.

species (SPEE-sheez)—any category of animals or plants that has many physical characteristics in common.

tumor (TOO-mur)—a growth on the body that is produced by rapid and abnormal production of cells.

uniformitarianism (YOO-nuh-for-meh-TAIR-ee-uh-nih-zum)—the belief that geologic formations have developed gradually over time.

For Further Reading

For Young Adults

Altman, Linda Jacobs. *Mr. Darwin's Voyage.* Parsippany, N.J.: Dillon Press, 1995.

Anderson, Margaret J. *Charles Darwin: Naturalist.* Hillside, N.J.: Enslow Publishers, 1994.

Parker, Steve. *Charles Darwin and Evolution.* Philadelphia: Chelsea House, 1995.

Sis, Peter. *The Tree of Life.* New York: Frances Foster Books, 2003.

Stefoff, Rebecca. *Charles Darwin and the Evolution Revolution.* New York: Oxford University Press, 1996.

Works Consulted

Allen, Bill. "From the Editor." *National Geographic,* November 2004.

Aydon, Cyril. *Charles Darwin.* New York: Carroll & Graf, 2002.

Bowlby, John. *Charles Darwin: A New Life.* New York: W. W. Norton, 1990.

Bragg, Melvyn. *On Giants' Shoulders: Great Scientists and Their Discoveries.* New York: John Wiley & Sons, 1998.

Darwin, Charles. *The Autobiography of Charles Darwin.* Edited by Nora Barlow. New York: W. W. Norton & Company, 1969.

———. *The Illustrated Origin of Species.* New York: Hill and Wang, 1979.

———. *The Voyage of Charles Darwin.* Selected and arranged by Christopher Ralling. New York: Mayflower Books, 1979.

Huxley, Julian, and H.B.D. Kettlewell. *Charles Darwin and His World.* New York: Viking Press, 1965.

Isaak, Mark. "What Is Creationism?" http://www.talkorigins.org/faqs/wic.html.

Nichols, Peter. *Evolution's Captain.* New York: HarperCollins, 2003.

Quammen, David. "Was Darwin Wrong?" *National Geographic,* November 2004.

On the Internet

American Experience: *Monkey Trial*
http://www.pbs.org/wgbh/amex/monkeytrial/index.html

Associated Press, "Evolution Reference Hurts Volcano Film." March 23, 2005.
http://www.movielords.com/3-evolution-reference-hurts-volcano-film.html

BBC Education: *Evolution Website*
http://www.bbc.co.uk/education/darwin/index.shtml

Bishop Ussher Dates the World: 4004 B.C.
http://www.lhup.edu/~dsimanek/ussher.htm

Collect Medical Antiques. "General Surgery & Amputation"
http://www.collectmedicalantiques.com/amputation3.html

Dean, Cornelia. "Evolution Takes a Back Seat in U.S. Classes." *New York Times,* February 1, 2005.
http://www.theocracywatch.org/schools_evolution_back_seat_times_jan1_05.htm

Following the Path of Discovery: "Robert Fitzroy"
http://www.juliantrubin.com/fitzroy.html

Geology
http://encarta.msn.com/text_761555455___66/Geology.html

Gibson, L. James. *Inherit the Wind—Revisited*
http://www.grisda.org/origins/51046.htm

Harrop, Froma. "Finding Common Ground Between God and Evolution." *Seattle Times,* January 25, 2005.
http://seattletimes.nwsource.com/html/opinion/2002159485_harrop25.html

An Introduction to the Scopes (Monkey) Trial
http://www.law.umkc.edu/faculty/projects/ftrials/scopes/evolut.htm

Isaak, Mark. "What Is Creationism?"
http://www.talkorigins.org/faqs/wic.html

PBS. *Evolution: A Journey into Where We're From and Where We're Going*
http://www.pbs.org/wgbh/evolution/index.html

The Scopes Monkey Trial
http://www3.mistral.co.uk/bradburyac/tennesse.html

USGS. "Age of the Earth"
http://pubs.usgs.gov/gip/geotime/age.html

Index

Age of the Earth 35
Atkinson, William 21
Becquerel, Henri 35
Boltwood, Bertram 35
Bryan, William Jennings 11
Buffon, Georges 35
Copernicus 41
Corfield, Richard 25
Darwin, Anne Elizabeth (daughter) 32
Darwin, Caroline (sister) 13, 14
Darwin, Catherine (sister) 13
Darwin, Charles
    Alfred Russel Wallace and 33
    Attends Cambridge 16–17
    Birth of 13
    Charles Darwin Research
        Station 22
    Childhood of 14
    Controversies and 7–10, 37, 41
    Death of 39
    Early education of 14–16
    Galapagos Islands and 22, 26, 30
    Illness of 25, 32, 34, 38
    Invited on *Beagle* voyage 17–19
    Marries Emma Wedgwood 31
    Studies barnacles 33, 34
    Theory of natural selection 30–31
    Works of
        Descent of Man, The 37–38
        Formation of Vegetable Mould Through the Action of Earthworms, The 38
        On the Origin of Species by Means of Natural Selection 7, 29, 33–34, 37, 38
        Naturalist's Voyage, A 32
Darwin, Emma Wedgwood (wife) 31, 38, 39
Darwin, Erasmus (brother) 12, 13, 14, 15
Darwin, Erasmus (grandfather) 13
Darwin, Marianne (sister) 13, 14

Darwin, Robert (father) 13, 14, 15, 16, 19, 31
Darwin, Susan (sister) 13, 14
Darwin, Susannah (mother) 13, 14
Darwin, William Erasmus (son) 32
Darrow, Clarence 11
Davy, Humphry 21
DeLay, Tom 9
Finches 26, 27, 30, 31
FitzRoy, Captain Robert 18, 19, 20, 23, 24, 25, 27
Gould, Stephen Jay 38–39
Henslow, John Stevens 16–17, 18, 24, 37
HMS *Beagle* 18, 20, 23, 24, 25, 26, 27, 29, 30
Hooker, Joseph 8, 34, 37
Humboldt, Alexander von 17
Huxley, Thomas 8, 37
Lightfoot, John 35
Long, Dr. Crawford 21
Lyell, Charles 23, 24, 37
Malthus, Thomas 30, 33
Matthews, Richard 24, 25
Mendel, Gregor 40, 41
Morton, Dr. William 21
Newton, Sir Isaac 39
Other Theories 10, 42
Owen, Richard 36, 37
Ptolemy 41
Scopes, John 11
Scopes Monkey Trial 9, 11
Sedgwick, Adam 17, 37
Stokes, Pringle 24
Tenerife 19, 23
Ussher, Bishop James 35
Victoria, Queen 21
Wallace, Alfred Russel 33, 34
Warren, Dr. John Charles 21
Wedgwood, Josiah (grandfather) 13
Wedgwood, Josiah (uncle) 19
Wells, Dr. Horace 21
Westminster Abbey 39, 40
Wilberforce, Bishop Samuel 7–8, 9, 39